INSTANT POT VEGAN COOKBOOK

THE SIMPLY VEGAN, FRESH, PLANT-BASED RECIPES FOR YOUR ELECTRIC PRESSURE COOKER

By Tina B.Baker

© **Copyright 2017 - All rights reserved.**

This document is geared towards providing exact and reliable information in regards to the topic and issue covered. The publication is sold on the idea that the publisher is not required to render an accounting, officially permitted, or otherwise, qualified services. If advice is necessary, legal or professional, a practiced individual in the profession should be ordered.

- From a Declaration of Principles which was accepted and approved equally by a Committee of the American Bar Association and a Committee of Publishers and Associations.

In no way is it legal to reproduce, duplicate, or transmit any part of this document by either electronic means or in printed format. Recording of this publication is strictly prohibited and any storage of this document is not allowed unless with written permission from the publisher. All rights reserved.

The information provided herein is stated to be truthful and consistent, in that any liability, regarding inattention or otherwise, by any usage or abuse of any policies, processes, or directions contained within is the solitary and utter responsibility of the recipient reader. Under no circumstances will any legal responsibility or blame be held against the publisher for any reparation, damages, or monetary loss due to the information herein, either directly or indirectly.

Respective authors own all copyrights not held by the publisher.

The information herein is offered for informational purposes solely and is universal as so. The presentation of the information is without a contract or any guarantee assurance.

The trademarks that are used are without any consent, and the publication of the trademark is without permission or backing by the trademark owner. All trademarks and brands within this book are for clarifying purposes only and are the owned by the owners themselves, not affiliated with this document.

CONTENTS

INTRODUCTION

CHAPTER 1: GETTING TO KNOW INSTANT POT

WHY INSTANT POT IS THE BEST FOR YOU

DIFFERENT COOKING SETTINGS TO GET FAMILIAR WITH

SPECIAL INSTANT POT FUNCTIONS

INSTANT POT: WHICH ONE TO BUY?

COOKING TIME CHARTS FOR All VEGAN INGREDIENTS

CHAPTER 2: VEGAN BREAKFAST RECIPES

Raisin Farro Breakfast

Classic Apple Oats

Instant Fruit Cobbler

Nutty Banana Oats

Black Bean Quinoa

Vanilla Walnut Oats

Potato Berry Breakfast

Soy Milk Apple Quinoa

CHAPTER 3: HEALTHY SIDES & APPETIZERS

Zucchini Potato Appetizer

Eggplant Tomatino

Spinach Tomato Appetizer

Chili Garlic Okra

CHAPTER 4: SUPER SOUPS, CURRIES & STEWS

Cashew Rice Soup

Quinoa Mixed Bean Soup

Broccoli Bean Soup

Corn Peppery Chowder

Sweet Potato Lemongrass Soup

Classic Lentil Potato Stew

Broccoli Cashew Soup

Kale Squash Stew

Zucchini Garlic Soup

Cauliflower Chickpea Soup

CHAPTER 5: GRAINS & RICE MEALS

Apple Almond Rice Meal

Multigrain Risotto

Garlic Bean Rice Meal

Avocado Rice Salad

Spinach Chickpea Rice Meal

Sorghum Pumpkin Meal

Spinach Mushroom Risotto

Green Tea Rice Risotto

CHAPTER 6: WHOLESOME VEGAN MAINS

Masala Kidney Beans

Spinach Jalapeno Lentil Curry

Creamy Lima Beans

Zucchini Eggplant Meal

Jalapeno Bean Meal

Wholesome Cauliflower Meal

Faro Peas Collard Wraps

Chili Bean Tacos

CHAPTER 7: SAVORY VEGAN SNACKS

Oregano Black Bean

Classic Potato Fries

Chickpea Hummus

Soy Sauce Tofu

CHAPTER 8: VEGAN SAUCES & SPREADS

Apple Mango Spread/Chutney

BBQ Sauce

Garlic Tomato Sauce

Pumpkin Butter

CHAPTER 9: DELICIOUS DESSERTS

Cashew Tapioca Pudding

Stuffed Dessert Apples

Berry Dessert Mystery

Buckwheat Banana Treat

CONCLUSION

Get Your Special Bonus For Free

SIGN UP HERE

www.bakerbooksworld.xyz

INTRODUCTION

With this While the world is terrorizing us with fancy new diseases and health disorders, the importance of achieving superior health has reached its peak. We care about our health as well as our family's health. While we cannot ignore the importance of nutrition in our diet, we also don't like to compromise on their deliciousness. It might be someone's viewpoint that you need to let go taste for nutrition, the modern invention called "Instant Pot" strongly denies that.

The Instant Pot is the modern kitchen solution to all your worries and hassles. It works on automation cooking technology that requires minimal human attention. This revolutionary cooking appliance generates high pressure steam through the electric heating source. With the help of this steam, it cooks food in quick time as compared to traditional cooking methods. You need to add ingredients to its cooking pot, set cooking time, set cooking mode, and your job is done. Instant Pot will now prepare delicious recipes for you in a matter of minutes.

This amazing kitchen appliance remembers to preserve nutrition. One great advantage of using an Instant Pot is that meals can be cooked quickly along with maintaining their nutritional values. The Vegan diet is enjoying unprecedented popularity across the world. The Vegan diet is becoming a solution to many health disorder and diseases as it prohibits ingredients having an animal origin.

While the usage of meats and dairy products are restricted, vegan diet mostly consists leafy greens, grains, pulses, cereals, beans, nuts, whole bread, seeds, fresh fruits, and spices. Vegan cuisines offer a smart combination of essential nutrients including protein, anti-oxidants, vitamins, and minerals. Instant Pot has been designed to cook nutrient-rich vegan meals for vegan enthusiasts.

In this dedicated Instant Pot cookbook, you can explore a hand-picked collection of 50 Vegan recipes divided into versatile chapters on breakfast, appetizers, sides, soups, stews, main course meals, snacks, sauces, and mouthwatering desserts.

Let's take a glance at what Instant Pot has to offer you for an ultimate cooking experience!

CHAPTER 1: GETTING TO KNOW INSTANT POT

WHY INSTANT POT IS THE BEST FOR YOU

Saves Time & Energy
Instant pot takes less time to prepare food as compared to other cooking methods. This appliance works particularly well with dried ingredients including beans, grains, legumes, and/or pulses. Instead of pre-soaking them for 2 to 12 hours prior to cooking time, you can directly add them to the pot, along with the recommended amount of liquids and other ingredients. At high pressure, you can cook them in less than 30 minutes.

Nutrition Health
Unlike many other cooking methods, which require you to fully immerse the vegetables and other ingredients under the water to cook them, instant pot needs just enough water to maintain high pressure the steam levels. This technique prevents essential ingredients from being washed away.

Cooking Convenience
An instant pot has 12-key functions which include poultry, rice, bean/chili, meat/ stew, soup, multi-grain, steam, porridges, and other control keys. Each mode has specifications for pressure and time, which can be adjusted as per your convenience.

Kills Micro-Organism
In instant pot, the water level is heated to a high temperature where most of the unwanted micro-organisms are killed off. It kills harmful bacteria and fungus from grains and vegetables to serve you with healthy meals every time.

DIFFERENT COOKING SETTINGS TO GET FAMILIAR WITH

Manual

With this function, you can manually set cooking time as per your requirements.

Steam

This Instant Pot cooking setting is used for steaming seafood, veggies or reheating foods. The default cooking time for this setting is 10 minutes on High Pressure setting.

Rice

This Instant Pot cooking setting coverts it into a rice cooker. The default cooking time for this setting is automatic on Low Pressure setting. You can use "Adjust" setting to increase or decrease cooking time as per your convenience.

Stew

This Instant Pot cooking setting is for making meats or stew. The default cooking time for this setting is 35 minutes on High Pressure setting.

Soup

This Instant Pot cooking setting is for making a variety of broths and soups. The default cooking time for this setting is 30 minutes on High Pressure setting.

Keep Warm/Cancel

This Instant Pot cooking setting is used to undo or cancel the exiting cooking setting. It does not turn off Instant Pot but puts it in a standby mode.

Bean/Chili

This Instant Pot cooking setting is for making chili or cooking beans. The default cooking time for this setting is 30 minutes on High Pressure setting.

Porridge

This Instant Pot cooking setting for making oatmeal or porridge using various grains. The default cooking time for this setting is 20 minutes on High Pressure setting.

Multigrain

This Instant Pot cooking setting is for making a mixture of grains such as brown rice, mung beans, wild rice, etc. The default cooking time for this setting is 20 minutes on High Pressure setting.

The 'MORE' setting is given for added cooking convenience; it provides 45 minutes of just warm water soaking which is followed by 2 hours of cooking time on High Pressure setting. The 'LESS' setting automatically sets 20 minutes of cooking time.

Sauté

This Instant Pot cooking setting is for open lid browning, sautéing or simmering of added ingredients. The most common of which are oil, onions, garlic, cumin seeds, spices, etc.

Yogurt

The default cooking time for this setting is 8 hours of incubation for different types of yogurts. You can use "Adjust" setting to increase or decrease time.

Slow Cook

This Instant Pot cooking setting coverts it into a slow cooker. It allows you to cook to up for 40 hours. The default cooking time for this setting is 4 hours.

SPECIAL INSTANT POT FUNCTIONS

NPR (Natural Pressure Release)

As the name states, NPR function is for naturally releasing pressure. It means that it slowly releases build up the pressure in the pot and it usually takes 10-15 minutes to release all inside pressure.

Leave the vent valve alone until it releases all inside pressure by its own. When all inside pressure gets released, the silver button on top of the lid goes down.

QPR (Quick Pressure Release)

As the name states, QPR function is for quickly releasing the build up pressure. Many recipes do not require natural pressure release, and they taste better when the pressure is released in a quickly.

Use a towel or some other clothing piece to cover the vent to diffuse anything that might come out due to a strong pressure of steam. Open the valve slowly a little at a time until the force reduces.

PIP (Pot in Pot)

PIP terminology is used when you need to add another container inside cooking pot area. With Instant Pot pressure cooking, the pot does not get as hot as an oven as you bake; that is the reason why you need to use stainless steel, glass, silicone cups or any other oven proof container to arrange inside the cooking pot area and then start the cooking process.

INSTANT POT: WHICH ONE TO BUY?

Lux

This model is available in the market in two popular sizes of 5 and 6 Quart. One disadvantage of the Lux model is that it cooks only on High Pressure setting and you can't cook any recipe with low pressure. However, it cooks most of the vegan recipes effortlessly.

It comes with various pre-set temperature setting; also you can use it as a rice cooker and slow cooker. Lux does not offer a yogurt making function. Some advanced Lux models are offering Bluetooth connectivity using its exclusive mobile app.

Duo

This model is available in the market in two popular sizes of 5 and 6 Quart. Duo is the most popular model among Instant Pot users. It offers the convenience of both high and low pressure cooking. It comes with various pre-set temperature setting; also you can use it as a rice cooker and slow cooker. Duo offers yogurt making function.

Some advanced Duo Plus models are offering Bluetooth connectivity through its exclusive mobile application. Duo Plus provides a unique feature of blue LCD screen and displays various cooking icons.

Smart

This model gives you more control over your cooking technique preference by offering many customized setting for your ultimate cooking comfort. This model offers 11 pre-set temperature setting, and you can set delay timer for up to 24 hours. It offers the convenience of both high and low pressure cooking. Also, you can use it as a rice cooker and slow cooker.

This model is available in the market with a standard size of 6 quart. Smart model offers yogurt making function. It has one special feature of cooking progress indicator.

COOKING TIME CHARTS FOR All VEGAN INGREDIENTS

Instant pot lets you cook all your favorite vegan ingredients in a matter of minutes. Following are time charts for different vegan ingredients.

- Rice and Grains
- Dry Beans, Legume and Lentils
- Fresh or Frozen Vegetable
- Fruits

Time Chart: Rice & Grains

Vegan Ingredient	Pressure Cooking Time (Minutes)	Ratio (Ingredient : Water)
Barley, pot	25 – 30	1:3 ~ 1:4
Barley, pearl	25-30	1:4
Millet	10 – 12	1:1 2/3
Quinoa, quick cooking	8	1:2
Corn, dried	25 – 30	1:3
Basmati rice	4-8	1: 1.5
Couscous	5 – 8	1:2
Brown rice	22-28	1: 1.25
White rice	8	1: 1.5
Congee, thin	15 – 20	1:6 ~ 1:7
Congee, thick	15 – 20	1:4 ~ 1:5
Sorghum	20-25	1:3
Kamut, whole	10 – 12	1:3
Oats, steel-cut	10	1:1 2/3
Porridge, thin	15-20	1:6 ~ 1:7
Oats, quick cooking	6	1:1 2/3
Wheat berries	25-30	1:3

Time Chart: Bean, Lentils & Legumes

Vegan Ingredient	Pressure Cooking Time for Soaked Variety (Minutes)	Pressure Cooking Time for Dry Variety (Minutes)
Black-eyed peas	10 – 15	20 – 25
White kidney beans	20 – 25	35 – 40
Pinto beans	20 – 25	25 – 30
Black beans	10 – 15	20 – 25
Red kidney beans	20 – 25	25 – 30
Peas	10 – 15	15-20
Chickpeas	20 – 25	35 – 40
Yellow Lentils	-	15 – 18
Navy beans	20 – 25	25 – 30
Red lentils	-	15 – 18
Cannellini beans	20 – 25	35 – 40
Lima beans	10 – 15	20 – 25
Green lentils	-	15 – 20
Soybeans	20 – 25	25 – 30

Time Chart: Vegetables

Vegan Ingredient	Pressure Cooking Time for Fresh Variety (Minutes)	Pressure Cooking Time for Frozen Variety (Minutes)
Collard	4 – 5	5 – 6
Zucchini	2 – 3	3-4
Celery, chunks	2 – 3	3 – 4
Endive	1-2	2-3
Cauliflower flowerets	2 – 3	3 – 4
Cabbage, red, purple or green, wedges	3 – 4	4 – 5
Carrots, whole or chunked	2 – 3	3 – 4
Carrots, sliced or shredded	1 – 2	2 – 3
Broccoli, flowerets	2 – 3	3 – 4
Trimmed Artichoke	9-11	11-13
Asparagus, whole or cut	1 – 2	2 – 3
Beans, green/yellow, whole, trim ends	1 – 2	2 – 3
Brussel sprouts, whole	3 – 4	4 – 5
Green beans, whole	2 – 3	3 – 4
Corn, on the cob	3 – 4	4 – 5
Corn, kernels	1 – 2	2 – 3
Eggplant, slices or chunks	2 – 3	3 – 4
Beets, small roots, whole	11 – 13	13 – 15
Whole Sweet Potatoes	10 – 12	15 – 19
Pumpkin, small slices or chunks	4 – 5	6 – 7
Rutabaga, slices	3 – 5	4-6
Potatoes, in cubes	7 – 9	9 – 11

Potatoes, whole, large	12 – 15	15 – 19
Okra	2 – 3	3 – 4
Tomatoes, in quarters	2 – 3	4 – 5
Sweet potato, in cubes	7 – 9	9 – 11
Mixed vegetables	2 – 3	3 – 4
Squash, acorn, slices or chunks	6 – 7	8 – 9
Leeks	2 – 4	3 – 5
Peas, green	1 – 2	2 – 3
Artichoke, hearts	4 – 5	5 – 6
Chopped greens including swiss chard, collards, kale, spinach, turnip greens	3 – 6	4 – 7

Time Chart: Fruits

Vegan Ingredient	Pressure Cooking Time for Fresh Variety (Minutes)	Pressure Cooking Time for Dried Variety (Minutes)
Apricots, whole or halves	2 – 3	3 – 4
Apples, in slices or pieces	2 – 3	3 – 4
Peaches	2 – 3	4 – 5
Raisins	N/A	4 – 5
Pears, slices or halves	2 – 3	4 – 5
Whole Apples	3-4	4-6
Prunes	2 – 3	4 – 5
Pears, whole	3 – 4	4 – 6

Chapter 2: Vegan Breakfast Recipes

Raisin Farro Breakfast

Prep Time: 5min.

Cooking Time: 5min.

Number of Servings: 3-4

Ingredients:

- 2 cups water
- ¼ cup brown sugar
- 1 cup farro
- 2 tablespoons vegetable oil
- 1 teaspoon vanilla extract
- ¼ teaspoon ground cinnamon
- ¼ cup raisins
- ¼ teaspoon salt
- chopped nuts of your choice

Directions:

1. Rinse the farro in a colander.
2. Take Instant Pot and carefully arrange it over a clean, dry kitchen platform. Turn on the appliance.
3. Find and press "Sauté" cooking function.
4. In the cooking pot area; add the oil and farro in the pot. Cook until turn fragrant. Add remainder of ingredients and stir again.
5. Close the pot lid and seal the valve to avoid any leakage. Find and press "Manual" cooking setting and set cooking time to 5 minutes.
6. Allow the recipe ingredients to cook for the set time, and after that, the timer reads "zero". Press "Cancel" and press "QPR" setting for quick pressure release.
7. Open the pot and arrange the cooked recipe in serving plates. Serve immediately topped with nuts and/or extra sugar.

Nutritional Values (Per Serving):

Calories - 203

Fat – 7g

Carbohydrates – 33g

Fiber – 2g

Protein – 4.5g

Classic Apple Oats

Prep Time: 5min.

Cooking Time: 5 min.

Number of Servings: 2

Ingredients:

- ½ teaspoon cinnamon
- ¼ teaspoon ginger
- 2 apples, make half-inch chunks
- ½ cup oats, steel cut
- 1 ½ cups water
- Maple syrup, as needed
- Pinch of salt
- Pinch of clove
- Pinch of nutmeg

Directions:

1. Take Instant Pot and carefully arrange it over a clean, dry kitchen platform. Turn on the appliance.
2. In the cooking pot area, add the water, oats, cinnamon, ginger, clove, nutmeg, apple and salt. Stir the ingredients gently.
3. Close the pot lid and seal the valve to avoid any leakage. Find and press "Manual" cooking setting and set cooking time to 5 minutes.
4. Allow the recipe ingredients to cook for the set time, and after that, the timer reads "zero".
5. Press "Cancel" and press "NPR" setting for natural pressure release. It takes 8-10 times for all inside pressure to release.
6. Open the pot and arrange the cooked recipe in serving plates.
7. Sweeten as needed with maple or agave syrup and serve immediately. Top with some chopped nuts, optional.

Nutritional Values (Per Serving):

Calories –248

Fat – 5.5g

Carbohydrates – 52g

Fiber – 13g

Protein – 7g

Instant Fruit Cobbler

Prep Time: 5min.

Cooking Time: 15 min.

Number of Servings: 2

Ingredients:

- 3 tablespoons coconut oil
- 2 tablespoons honey
- ½ teaspoon cinnamon
- 1 apple, sliced
- 1 plum, sliced
- 1 pear, sliced
- ¼ cup shredded unsweetened coconut
- ½ cup pecans, chopped

Directions:

1. Take Instant Pot and carefully arrange it over a clean, dry kitchen platform. Turn on the appliance.
2. In the cooking pot area, add the mentioned ingredients except for coconut and pecans. Stir the ingredients gently.
3. Close the pot lid and seal the valve to avoid any leakage. Find and press "Steam" cooking setting and set cooking time to 10 minutes.
4. Allow the recipe ingredients to cook for the set time and after that, the timer reads "zero".
5. Press "Cancel" and press "NPR" setting for natural pressure release. It takes 8-10 times for all inside pressure to release.
6. Open the pot and take out the cooked ingredients in a bowl; keep the cooking liquid inside the pot.
7. Add the pecans and coconut with the cooking liquid; mix well. Using the sauté setting, cook for about five minutes while occasionally stirring until turn browned.
8. Add in serving plates and sprinkle the nut mixture over the fruit mixture. Enjoy!

Nutritional Values (Per Serving):

Calories – 409

Fat – 32g

Carbohydrates – 38g

Fiber – 9g

Protein – 3g

Nutty Banana Oats

Prep Time: 5min.

Cooking Time: 3 min.

Number of Servings: 2

Ingredients:

- 2 sliced bananas
- 3 cups water
- 1 teaspoon ground cinnamon
- 1 cup oats, steel cut
- Pinch of ground nutmeg
- Maple syrup, as needed
- ½ cup chopped nuts (almonds, walnuts, pecans, etc.)

Directions:

1. Take Instant Pot and carefully arrange it over a clean, dry kitchen platform. Turn on the appliance.
2. In the cooking pot area, add the water, oats, cinnamon, ginger, and half of the sliced banana. Stir the ingredients gently.
3. Close the pot lid and seal the valve to avoid any leakage. Find and press "Manual" cooking setting and set cooking time to 3 minutes.
4. Allow the recipe ingredients to cook for the set time and after that, the timer reads "zero".
5. Press "Cancel" and press "NPR" setting for natural pressure release. It takes 8-10 times for all inside pressure to release.
6. Open the pot and arrange the cooked recipe in serving plates. Top with leftover banana and nuts, and enjoy the vegan recipe!

Nutritional Values (Per Serving):

Calories - 296

Fat – 9g

Carbohydrates – 42.5g

Fiber – 8g

Protein – 10g

Black Bean Quinoa

Prep Time: 8-10min.

Cooking Time: 20 min.

Number of Servings: 4

Ingredients:

- 1/2 teaspoon salt
- 1 bell pepper, diced
- 1 teaspoon ground cumin
- 1 teaspoon olive oil, extra-virgin
- 1 cup water
- 1/2 red onion, diced
- 1 cup quinoa, rinse and drain
- 1 cup prepared salsa
- 1 1/2 cups black beans, cooked

Directions:

1. Take Instant Pot and carefully arrange it over a clean, dry kitchen platform. Turn on the appliance.
2. Find and press "Sauté" cooking function.
3. In the cooking pot area; add the oil, peppers, and onions in the pot. Cook for 6-8 minutes to cook well and soften.
4. Mix in the cumin and salt; cook for 1 more minute. Mix in the salsa, bean, quinoa, and water.
5. Close the pot lid and seal the valve to avoid any leakage. Find and press "Manual" cooking setting and set cooking time to 12 minutes.
6. Allow the recipe ingredients to cook for the set time and after that, the timer reads "zero".
7. Press "Cancel" and press "NPR" setting for natural pressure release. It takes 8-10 times for all inside pressure to release.
8. Open the pot; fluff the quinoa and arrange the cooked recipe in serving plates.
9. Top with some of your favorite toppings such as salsa, diced onions, lettuce, sliced avocado, etc. Enjoy the vegan recipe!

Nutritional Values (Per Serving):

Calories - 272

Fat – 6g

Carbohydrates – 38.5g

Fiber – 17.5g

Protein – 10g

Vanilla Walnut Oats

Prep Time: 5 min.

Cooking Time: 3 min.

Number of Servings: 4

Ingredients:

- 1 cup steel-cut oats
- ½ vanilla bean
- 1 cinnamon stick
- 1 cup unsweetened, almond or soy milk
- 2 cup water
- Pinch of salt
- ¼ cup raisins or walnut
- 1 teaspoon ground cinnamon
- ½ tablespoon maple syrup
- ¼ cup toasted walnuts

Directions:

1. Take Instant Pot and carefully arrange it over a clean, dry kitchen platform. Turn on the appliance.
2. In the cooking pot area, add the oats, salt, milk, water, cinnamon stick, and ¼ cup of raisins. Stir the ingredients gently.
3. Close the pot lid and seal the valve to avoid any leakage. Find and press "Manual" cooking setting and set cooking time to 3 minutes.
4. Allow the recipe ingredients to cook for the set time and after that, the timer reads "zero".
5. Press "Cancel" and press "NPR" setting for natural pressure release. It takes 8-10 times for all inside pressure to release.
6. Open the pot and discard the cinnamon stick and vanilla bean. Set aside.
7. Stir well, and mix in the walnuts, cinnamon, and rest of the raisins.
8. Add sweetener and serve warm!

Nutritional Values (Per Serving):

Calories - 204

Fat – 9g

Carbohydrates – 19.5g

Fiber – 3g

Protein – 7g

Potato Berry Breakfast

Prep Time: 10min.

Cooking Time: 20-30 min.

Number of Servings: 4

Ingredients:

- 2 medium potatoes, cubed
- 2 medium onions, sliced
- 2 cups white wheat berries, soaked overnight
- 5 stalks celery, sliced
- 3 smashed garlic cloves (optional)
- 1 tbs. vegan butter
- 1 tbs. salt
- 2 cups sliced carrots
- 6 1/2 cups water
- 1 teaspoon seasoning of your choice
- 1/8 teaspoon thyme

Directions:

1. Take Instant Pot and carefully arrange it over a clean, dry kitchen platform. Turn on the appliance.

2. Find and press "Sauté" cooking function.

3. In the cooking pot area; add the butter, garlic, celery, and onions in the pot. Cook for 2 minutes to cook well and soften.

4. Transfer the mixture in separate bowl; set aside.

5. In the cooking pot area, add the berries, potatoes, and carrots. Stir the ingredients gently.

6. Close the pot lid and seal the valve to avoid any leakage. Find and press "Multigrain" cooking setting. It will set cooking time automatically.

7. Allow the recipe ingredients to cook for the set time, and after that, the timer reads "zero".

8. Press "Cancel" and press "NPR" setting for natural pressure release. It takes 8-10 times for all inside pressure to release.

9. Open the pot and add the sautéed mixture.

10. Add the seasoning, thyme, and salt. Simmer the mixture for 25-30 minutes and serve warm!

Nutritional Values (Per Serving):

Calories –432

Fat – 5.2g

Carbohydrates – 55g

Fiber – 14g

Protein – 14.5g

Soy Milk Apple Quinoa

Prep Time: 10min.

Cooking Time: 1 min.

Number of Servings: 4

Ingredients:

- ¼ cup brown sugar
- ¼ teaspoon cinnamon powder
- ½ cup apple, peeled & make slices of ½-inch thick
- ½ cup apple, peeled &diced
- ½ cup soy milk
- 2 cups water
- 1 cup brown or red quinoa, rinsed & drained
- ¼ teaspoon squeezed lemon juice

Directions:

1. In a bowl of medium size, add the apples and top with the lemon juice. Set aside and drain the liquid.
2. Take Instant Pot and carefully arrange it over a clean, dry kitchen platform. Turn on the appliance.
3. In the cooking pot area, add the ingredients except for garnishes and milk. Stir the ingredients gently.
4. Close the pot lid and seal the valve to avoid any leakage. Find and press "Manual" cooking setting and set cooking time to 1 minutes.
5. Allow the recipe ingredients to cook for the set time and after that, the timer reads "zero".
6. Press "Cancel" and press "NPR" setting for natural pressure release. It takes 8-10 times for all inside pressure to release.
7. Open the pot and pour in the milk and season as needed.
8. Add equal portions of quinoa into serving bowls. Garnish with a few slices of apples. Serve warm!

Nutritional Values (Per Serving):

Calories – 212

Fat – 3g

Carbohydrates – 48.5g

Fiber – 4.5g

Protein – 2g

Chapter 3: Healthy Sides & Appetizers

Zucchini Potato Appetizer

Prep Time: 5min.

Cooking Time: 10 min.

Number of Servings: 6-7

Ingredients:

- 1 bell pepper, cubed
- 6 cherry tomatoes, halved
- 1 large potato, cubed
- 1 zucchini, make thick rounds
- 1 onion, make small wedges
- A handful pine nuts
- 1/2 tablespoon raisins, soaked in water
- 1 cup basil, chopped
- 1 large eggplant, cubed
- 1/4 cup olive oil
- 1/2 tablespoon capers
- 2 tablespoons green olives, pitted
- Pepper and salt as needed

Directions:

1. Add the salt over eggplant cubes and arrange in a strainer for 25-30 minutes.
2. Take Instant Pot and carefully arrange it over a clean, dry kitchen platform. Turn on the appliance.
3. Find and press "Sauté" cooking function.
4. In the cooking pot area; add the oil and eggplant cubes in the pot. Cook for 2-3 minutes to cook well and soften.
5. Add the onion and some pepper; sauté until translucent.
6. Add rest the ingredients and cook for 2-3 more minutes. Add 1/2 cup water, salt, and some pepper.
7. Close the pot lid and seal the valve to avoid any leakage. Find and press "Manual" cooking setting and set cooking time to 4 minutes.

8. Allow the recipe ingredients to cook for the set time and after that, the timer reads "zero".
9. Press "Cancel" and press "NPR" setting for natural pressure release. It takes 8-10 times for all inside pressure to release.
10. Open the pot and arrange the cooked recipe in serving plates. Enjoy the vegan recipe!

Nutritional Values (Per Serving):

Calories - 441

Fat – 16g

Carbohydrates – 60.5g

Fiber – 8g

Protein – 6g

Eggplant Tomatino

Prep Time: 5min.

Cooking Time: 4 min.

Number of Servings: 6-7

Ingredients:

- 2 ½ pounds eggplant, make 1-inch cubes
- 7 ½ ounces canned tomato sauce
- 2 cans (16 ounces each) diced tomatoes with its juice
- 4 celery stalks, make 1-inch pieces
- 2 large onions, thinly sliced
- 2 tablespoons olive oil, divided
- 2 tablespoons capers, drained
- 1 tablespoon maple syrup
- 1 cup olives, pitted and halved
- 4 tablespoons balsamic vinegar
- 2 teaspoons dried basil
- Pepper and salt as needed
- Basil leaves to garnish

Directions:

1. Take Instant Pot and carefully arrange it over a clean, dry kitchen platform. Turn on the appliance.
2. In the cooking pot area, add the mentioned ingredients. Stir the ingredients gently.
3. Close the pot lid and seal the valve to avoid any leakage. Find and press "Manual" cooking setting and set cooking time to 4 minutes.
4. Allow the recipe ingredients to cook for the set time, and after that, the timer reads "zero". Press "Cancel" and press "QPR" setting for quick pressure release.
5. Open the pot and arrange the cooked recipe in serving plates. Garnish with fresh basil and serve.

Nutritional Values (Per Serving):

Calories - 129

Fat – 6g

Carbohydrates – 18.5g

Fiber – 7g

Protein – 3g

Spinach Tomato Appetizer

Prep Time: 5min.

Cooking Time: 10-12 min.

Number of Servings: 4

Ingredients:

- 2 teaspoons garlic, minced
- 10 cups fresh spinach, chopped
- 1 ½ cups vegetable broth
- 1 tablespoon lemon juice
- 1 cup tomatoes, chopped
- ½ cup tomato puree
- 2 tablespoons olive oil
- 2 small onions, chopped
- ½ teaspoon red pepper flakes, crushed
- Pepper and salt as needed

Directions:

1. Take Instant Pot and carefully arrange it over a clean, dry kitchen platform. Turn on the appliance.
2. Find and press "Sauté" cooking function.
3. In the cooking pot area; add the oil and onions in the pot. Cook for 2-3 minutes to cook well and soften.
4. Add the garlic and red pepper flakes and cook for 1 minute. Add spinach and cook for 2 minutes.
5. In the cooking pot area, add the remaining ingredients. Stir the ingredients gently.
6. Close the pot lid and seal the valve to avoid any leakage. Find and press "Manual" cooking setting and set cooking time to 6 minutes.
7. Allow the recipe ingredients to cook for the set time, and after that, the timer reads "zero". Press "Cancel" and press "QPR" setting for quick pressure release.
8. Open the pot and arrange the cooked recipe in serving plates. Enjoy the vegan recipe!

Nutritional Values (Per Serving):

Calories - 168

Fat – 9g

Carbohydrates – 12g

Fiber – 3.5g

Protein – 10g

Chili Garlic Okra

Prep Time: 8-10min.

Cooking Time: 7-8 min.

Number of Servings: 4

Ingredients:

- 1 teaspoon cumin seeds
- 2 medium onions, sliced
- 2 medium tomatoes, chopped
- 2-pound okra, cut into 1-inch pieces
- ½ cup vegetable broth
- 1 teaspoon ground coriander
- ½ teaspoon red chili powder
- ½ teaspoon ground turmeric
- 2 tablespoons olive oil
- 6 garlic cloves, chopped
- Pepper and salt as needed

Directions:

1. Take Instant Pot and carefully arrange it over a clean, dry kitchen platform. Turn on the appliance.
2. Find and press "Sauté" cooking function.
3. In the cooking pot area; add the oil, cumin seeds, and garlic in the pot. Cook for 1 minutes to cook well and soften.
4. Add the onion and cook for 4 minutes. Add the remaining ingredients and cook for 1 more minute.
5. Close the pot lid and seal the valve to avoid any leakage. Find and press "Manual" cooking setting and set cooking time to 2 minutes.
6. Allow the recipe ingredients to cook for the set time, and after that, the timer reads "zero". Press "Cancel" and press "QPR" setting for quick pressure release.
7. Open the pot and arrange the cooked recipe in serving plates. Enjoy the vegan recipe!

Nutritional Values (Per Serving):

Calories –196

Fat – 8g

Carbohydrates – 26.5g

Fiber – 9g

Protein – 6.5g

Chapter 4: Super Soups, Curries & Stews

Cashew Rice Soup

Prep Time: 8-10min.

Cooking Time: 45 min.

Number of Servings: 7-8

Ingredients:

- 3 cloves garlic, minced
- 1 ½ cups carrots, chopped
- 1 ½ cups onion, chopped
- 1 tablespoon olive oil
- 2 bay leaves
- 1 ½ cups wild rice
- 1 ½ cups celery stalks, chopped
- 1 ½ cups dried chickpeas, soaked in water overnight
- 1 ½ teaspoons dried thyme
- 7 ½ cups vegetable broth
- 1 cup water
- ¾ cup raw cashew, soaked in hot water for 30 minutes
- Pepper and salt as needed

Directions:

1. Take Instant Pot and carefully arrange it over a clean, dry kitchen platform. Turn on the appliance.
2. Find and press "Sauté" cooking function.
3. In the cooking pot area; add the oil and onions in the pot. Cook for 2 minutes to cook well and soften.
4. Stir in the garlic and sauté until fragrant. Stir in the carrots and celery and sauté for a couple of minutes.
5. Add the chickpeas, bay leaf, wild rice, thyme, and broth.
6. Close the pot lid and seal the valve to avoid any leakage. Find and press "Manual" cooking setting and set cooking time to 35 minutes.

7. Allow the recipe ingredients to cook for the set time, and after that, the timer reads "zero".
8. Press "Cancel" and press "NPR" setting for natural pressure release. It takes 8-10 times for all inside pressure to release.
9. Open the pot.
10. Add cashew and water to a blender and blend until smooth. Add the mix to the Instant Pot and combine well.
11. Mix the pepper and salt. Ladle into soup bowls and serve.

Nutritional Values (Per Serving):

Calories - 394

Fat – 11.5g

Carbohydrates – 52g

Fiber – 10.5g

Protein – 19g

Quinoa Mixed Bean Soup

Prep Time: 5min.

Cooking Time: 2 min.

Number of Servings: 3

Ingredients:

- 1 cup kidney beans or pinto beans
- 7.5 oz. canned diced tomatoes
- 1/4 tablespoon dried oregano
- Pepper and salt as needed
- 1/2 tablespoon dried basil
- 1/2 tablespoon hot sauce
- 2 tablespoons quinoa rinsed
- 1/2 tablespoon garlic, minced
- 6 oz. frozen vegetables
- 7.5 oz. cannelloni beans
- 1/2 teaspoon onion powder
- 1 1/2 cups boiling water

Directions:

1. Take Instant Pot and carefully arrange it over a clean, dry kitchen platform. Turn on the appliance.
2. In the cooking pot area, add the mentioned ingredients. Stir the ingredients gently.
3. Close the pot lid and seal the valve to avoid any leakage. Find and press "Manual" cooking setting and set cooking time to 2 minutes.
4. Allow the recipe ingredients to cook for the set time, and after that, the timer reads "zero".
5. Press "Cancel" and press "NPR" setting for natural pressure release. It takes 8-10 times for all inside pressure to release.
6. Open the pot and arrange the cooked recipe in serving plates. Enjoy the vegan recipe!

Nutritional Values (Per Serving):

Calories –345

Fat – 9g

Carbohydrates – 52g

Fiber – 22g

Protein – 21.5g

Broccoli Bean Soup

Prep Time: 5min.

Cooking Time: 5 min.

Number of Servings: 6

Ingredients:

- 1 cup shredded cabbage
- 1 cup broccoli florets
- ½ cup kidney beans
- 1 teaspoon oregano
- 1 tablespoon soy sauce
- 1 teaspoon onion powder
- ¼ cup quinoa
- 1 tablespoon vegetable oil
- 4 garlic cloves, minced
- 1 cup carrots, chopped
- 1 cup green bell pepper, chopped
- 4 cups vegetable broth
- ¼ teaspoon salt
- 2 tablespoons lemon juice
- Some ground pepper
- Some basil leaves

Directions:

1. Take Instant Pot and carefully arrange it over a clean, dry kitchen platform. Turn on the appliance.
2. Find and press "Sauté" cooking function. Heat the vegetable oil. Add minced garlic and sauté for about a minute.
3. Add remaining ingredients to the pot slowly, except for basil leaves and pepper. Stir to mix well.
4. Close the pot lid and seal the valve to avoid any leakage. Find and press "Manual" cooking setting and set cooking time to 5 minutes.
5. Allow the recipe ingredients to cook for the set time, and after that, the timer reads "zero".

6. Press "Cancel" and press "NPR" setting for natural pressure release. It takes 8-10 times for all inside pressure to release.
7. Open the pot and arrange the cooked recipe in serving plates. Season with some ground pepper and garnish with basil leaves.

Nutritional Values (Per Serving):

Calories - 153

Fat – 4g

Carbohydrates – 21g

Fiber – 4.5g

Protein – 9g

Corn Peppery Chowder

Prep Time: 5min.

Cooking Time: 35 min.

Number of Servings: 4

Ingredients:

- 4 cups corn kernels
- 1 medium yellow onions, chopped
- 2 tablespoons olive oil
- 4 cups vegetable broth
- ½ teaspoon smoked paprika
- 1 teaspoon ground cumin
- 1 medium red bell peppers, chopped
- 3 medium gold potatoes, chopped
- ⅛ teaspoon cayenne pepper
- 1 cup almond milk
- Pepper as needed
- 1 scallion, chopped, to garnish

Directions:

1. Take Instant Pot and carefully arrange it over a clean, dry kitchen platform. Turn on the appliance.
2. Find and press "Sauté" cooking function.
3. In the cooking pot area; add the oil and onions in the pot. Cook for 2 minutes to cook well and soften.
4. Add the red bell pepper, 1 cup corn, potatoes, broth, salt, and spices.
5. Close the pot lid and seal the valve to avoid any leakage. Find and press "Manual" cooking setting and set cooking time to 15 minutes.
6. Allow the recipe ingredients to cook for the set time, and after that, the timer reads "zero".
7. Press "Cancel" and press "NPR" setting for natural pressure release. It takes 8-10 times for all inside pressure to release.
8. Open the pot. Blend in a blender until smooth. Add it back into the pot.
9. Add the remaining corn and almond milk.

10. Find and press "Sauté" cooking function; simmer for 15 minutes. Add the pepper and salt as needed and mixed well.
11. Ladle into soup bowls. Garnish with the scallions and red bell pepper.

Nutritional Values (Per Serving):

Calories - 364

Fat – 10.5g

Carbohydrates – 54.5g

Fiber – 7g

Protein – 12.5g

Sweet Potato Lemongrass Soup

Prep Time: 8-10min.

Cooking Time: 15 min.

Number of Servings: 7-8

Ingredients:

- 2 cups sweet potatoes, peeled and chopped
- 4 cups vegetable broth
- 1 red chili, chopped
- 4 stalks lemongrass, halved
- 6 large carrots, peeled and chopped
- 2 large celery stalks, chopped
- 2 medium onions, chopped
- 2 cups coconut milk
- 4 cloves garlic, pressed
- 1-inch piece of ginger, minced
- Salt as needed
- Juice of a lime
- Cilantro leaves, chopped, to garnish
- Sesame seeds to garnish

Directions:

1. Take Instant Pot and carefully arrange it over a clean, dry kitchen platform. Turn on the appliance.
2. In the cooking pot area, add the mentioned ingredients. Stir the ingredients gently.
3. Close the pot lid and seal the valve to avoid any leakage. Find and press "Soup" cooking setting and set cooking time to 15 minutes.
4. Allow the recipe ingredients to cook for the set time, and after that, the timer reads "zero". Press "Cancel" and press "QPR" setting for quick pressure release.
5. Open the pot and discard lemongrass.
6. Cool for a while and blend with a hand blender. Add the lime juice while blending.
7. Ladle into bowls. Garnish with the cilantro and sesame seeds.

Nutritional Values (Per Serving):

Calories –247

Fat – 15g

Carbohydrates – 24.5g

Fiber – 5g

Protein – 5.5g

Classic Lentil Potato Stew

Prep Time: 5min.

Cooking Time: 25-30 min.

Number of Servings: 4

Ingredients:

- 1 small stalk celery, chopped
- 2 cups Swiss chard, chopped
- ½ tablespoon soy sauce
- 1 clove garlic, minced
- 1 ½ cups lentils, rinsed
- 2 medium gold potatoes, cubed
- 1 ½ tablespoons olive oil
- 1 medium onion, chopped
- 1 medium carrot, sliced
- 3 cups vegetable broth
- Pepper and salt as needed

Directions:

1. Take Instant Pot and carefully arrange it over a clean, dry kitchen platform. Turn on the appliance.
2. Find and press "Sauté" cooking function.
3. In the cooking pot area; add the oil, garlic, stems of Swiss chard, celery, and onions in the pot.
4. Add the rest of the ingredients except the Swiss chard leaves and stir.
5. Close the pot lid and seal the valve to avoid any leakage. Find and press "Soup" cooking setting with default cooking time.
6. Allow the recipe ingredients to cook for the set time, and after that, the timer reads "zero".
7. Press "Cancel" and press "NPR" setting for natural pressure release. It takes 8-10 times for all inside pressure to release.
8. Open the pot and add the Swiss chard leaves.
9. Press "saute" and simmer until the chard wilts. Ladle into soup bowls and serve.

Nutritional Values (Per Serving):

Calories - 406

Fat – 8g

Carbohydrates – 58g

Fiber – 9.5g

Protein – 23.5g

Broccoli Cashew Soup

Prep Time: 5min.

Cooking Time: 25 min.

Number of Servings: 3

Ingredients:

- 1 cup broccoli, chopped into florets
- ½ teaspoon salt
- 6 tablespoons raw cashew, soaked in water for 4 hours
- 1 medium onion, chopped
- 2 medium carrots, chopped
- 2 cloves garlic, minced
- 3 cups water, divided
- 1 teaspoon olive oil
- 1 stalk celery, chopped
- Ground pepper as needed

Directions:

1. Take Instant Pot and carefully arrange it over a clean, dry kitchen platform. Turn on the appliance.
2. Find and press "Sauté" cooking function.
3. In the cooking pot area; add the oil, salt, and onions in the pot. Cook for 2 minutes to cook well and soften.
4. Stir in the carrots and celery and sauté for 2–3 minutes. Add the garlic and broccoli and sauté for a couple of minutes. Add 2 ½ cups water, pepper and salt.
5. Close the pot lid and seal the valve to avoid any leakage. Find and press "Soup" cooking setting and set cooking time to 20 minutes.
6. Allow the recipe ingredients to cook for the set time, and after that, the timer reads "zero".
7. Press "Cancel" and press "NPR" setting for natural pressure release. It takes 8-10 times for all inside pressure to release.
8. Open the pot and cool down the mix.
9. Blend it in a blender until smooth. Transfer the mix to a bowl.
10. Add the cashew into the blender with ½ cup water and blend until smooth. Pour into the soup mix and adjust seasoning and serve!

Nutritional Values (Per Serving):

Calories - 168

Fat – 9.5g

Carbohydrates – 18g

Fiber – 4g

Protein – 5.5g

Kale Squash Stew

Prep Time: 8-10min.

Cooking Time: 15 min.

Number of Servings: 6

Ingredients:

- 2 15-ounce can navy beans
- 2 teaspoons smoked paprika
- 1 teaspoon dried basil
- 2 teaspoons dried oregano
- 1 teaspoon cumin
- 6 cloves garlic, minced
- 1 tablespoon vegetable oil
- 1 large onion, chopped
- 1 red bell pepper, chopped
- 1 15-ounce can diced tomatoes
- ½ cup cilantro leaves
- 1 pound winter squash, peeled and cubed
- 1 bunch of kale
- 1 teaspoon salt
- 5 cups water

Directions:

1. Remove the kale stems and finely slice. Tear the leaves into bits.
2. Take Instant Pot and carefully arrange it over a clean, dry kitchen platform. Turn on the appliance.
3. Find and press "Sauté" cooking function.
4. In the cooking pot area; add the oil and onions in the pot. Cook for 2 minutes to cook well and soften.
5. Add the garlic and cook until fragrant. Add everything else except cilantro.
6. Close the pot lid and seal the valve to avoid any leakage. Find and press "Manual" cooking setting and set cooking time to 10 minutes.
7. Allow the recipe ingredients to cook for the set time, and after that, the timer reads "zero".

8. Press "Cancel" and press "NPR" setting for natural pressure release. It takes 8-10 times for all inside pressure to release.
9. Open the pot.
10. Add cilantro and let stand 10 minutes before serving.

Nutritional Values (Per Serving):

Calories - 337

Fat – 5g

Carbohydrates – 57.5g

Fiber – 24g

Protein – 19.5g

Zucchini Garlic Soup

Prep Time: 5-8 min.

Cooking Time: 20 min.

Number of Servings: 7-8

Ingredients:

- 1 tablespoon coconut oil or ghee
- 4 cloves garlic, sliced
- 5 medium zucchinis, make small chunks
- 2 onions, quartered
- 6 cups vegetable stock
- ½ cup coconut milk
- Ground pepper and salt as needed

Directions:

1. Take Instant Pot and carefully arrange it over a clean, dry kitchen platform. Turn on the appliance.
2. Find and press "Sauté" cooking function.
3. In the cooking pot area; add the oil, onions, zucchini, and garlic in the pot. Cook for 4-5 minutes to cook well and soften.
4. Add remaining ingredients except for coconut milk.
5. Close the pot lid and seal the valve to avoid any leakage. Find and press "Soup" cooking setting and set cooking time to 15 minutes.
6. Allow the recipe ingredients to cook for the set time, and after that, the timer reads "zero".
7. Press "Cancel" and press "NPR" setting for natural pressure release. It takes 8-10 times for all inside pressure to release.
8. Open the pot and add the coconut milk. Thoroughly blend the mixture with an immersion blender and serve warm!

Nutritional Values (Per Serving):

Calories - 89

Fat – 6g

Carbohydrates – 8g

Fiber – 3g

Protein – 1.5g

Cauliflower Chickpea Soup

Prep Time: 5min.

Cooking Time: 10 min.

Number of Servings: 8

Ingredients:

- 1 15-ounce can tomatoes, diced
- 1 teaspoon salt
- 1 tablespoon peanut butter
- ¼ teaspoon cayenne
- 3 cups water
- 1 large cauliflower head
- 1 15-ounce can chickpeas
- Pinch of cinnamon
- 1 pound sweet potato, diced
- 4 cloves garlic, minced
- 1 tablespoon grated ginger
- 1 tablespoon curry seasoning
- 1 jalapeno, seeded and minced
- 4 cups vegetable broth
- 1 large onion, chopped

Directions:

1. Take Instant Pot and carefully arrange it over a clean, dry kitchen platform. Turn on the appliance.
2. Find and press "Sauté" cooking function.
3. In the cooking pot area; add the oil and onions in the pot. Cook for 3 minutes to cook well and soften.
4. Add the garlic and cook for 1 minute. Add the broth, potatoes, curry, and cinnamon.
5. Close the pot lid and seal the valve to avoid any leakage. Find and press "Manual" cooking setting and set cooking time to 5 minutes.
6. Allow the recipe ingredients to cook for the set time, and after that, the timer reads "zero". Press "Cancel" and press "QPR" setting for quick pressure release.
7. Open the pot and

8. Add everything else except peanut butter.
9. Close the pot lid and seal the valve to avoid any leakage. Find and press "Manual" cooking setting and set cooking time to 1 minutes.
10. Allow the recipe ingredients to cook for the set time, and after that, the timer reads "zero".
11. Press "Cancel" and press "NPR" setting for natural pressure release. It takes 8-10 times for all inside pressure to release.
12. Stir in peanut butter and serve.

Nutritional Values (Per Serving):

Calories - 324

Fat – 5g

Carbohydrates – 46.5g

Fiber – 16g

Protein – 15g

Chapter 5: Grains & Rice Meals

Apple Almond Rice Meal

Prep Time: 8-10min.

Cooking Time: 35 min.

Number of Servings: 6

Ingredients:

- 1 chopped pear
- 3 ½ cups water
- 1 ½ cups wild rice
- 1 cup dried, mixed fruit
- 2 small apples, peeled and chopped
- ½ cup almonds, slivered
- 2 tablespoons apple juice
- 1 teaspoon cinnamon
- 1 tablespoon maple syrup
- 1 teaspoon veggie oil
- ½ teaspoon ground nutmeg
- Pepper and salt as needed

Directions:

1. Take Instant Pot and carefully arrange it over a clean, dry kitchen platform. Turn on the appliance.
2. In the cooking pot area, add the rice and water. Stir the ingredients gently.
3. Close the pot lid and seal the valve to avoid any leakage. Find and press "Manual" cooking setting and set cooking time to 30 minutes.
4. Allow the recipe ingredients to cook for the set time, and after that, the timer reads "zero".
5. Meanwhile, soak the dried fruit in just enough apple juice to cover everything in a bowl. Set aside for 30 minutes and then drain the fruit.
6. Press "Cancel" and press "NPR" setting for natural pressure release. It takes 8-10 times for all inside pressure to release.
7. Open the pot and transfer the mixture to serving bowl.

8. Find and press "Sauté" cooking function.
9. In the cooking pot area; add the oil, apples, pears, and almonds in the pot. Cook for 2 minutes to cook well and soften.
10. Mix in 2 tablespoon apple juice and keep cooking for a few minutes more. Mix in the syrup, cooked rice, soaked fruit, and seasonings.
11. Cook for 2-3 minutes and serve warm!

Nutritional Values (Per Serving):

Calories - 224

Fat – 3g

Carbohydrates – 38g

Fiber – 5.5g

Protein – 6.5g

Multigrain Risotto

Prep Time: 5min.

Cooking Time: 20-22 min.

Number of Servings: 6

Ingredients:

- 1 cup mixture of quinoa, millet, bulgur, oats, and buckwheat, or any other grains of your choice, soaked in water overnight, drained
- 1 cup coconut milk
- 4 cups water
- Sweetener as needed (optional)

Directions:

1. Take Instant Pot and carefully arrange it over a clean, dry kitchen platform. Turn on the appliance.
2. In the cooking pot area, add the mentioned ingredients. Stir the ingredients gently.
3. Close the pot lid and seal the valve to avoid any leakage. Find and press "Porridge" cooking setting with default cooking time.
4. Allow the recipe ingredients to cook for the set time, and after that, the timer reads "zero".
5. Press "Cancel" and press "NPR" setting for natural pressure release. It takes 8-10 times for all inside pressure to release.
6. Open the pot and arrange the cooked recipe in serving plates. Enjoy the vegan recipe!

Nutritional Values (Per Serving):

Calories - 191

Fat – 10.5g

Carbohydrates – 22.5g

Fiber – 3g

Protein – 4.5g

Garlic Bean Rice Meal

Prep Time: 10 min.

Cooking Time: 25 min.

Number of Servings: 4

Ingredients:

- 2 tablespoons olive oil
- 2 cloves garlic, minced
- 1 cup brown rice, rinsed
- 1 cup black beans, rinsed
- 1 medium onion, chopped
- 4 ½ cups water
- ½ avocado, sliced to serve
- Salt as needed
- 2 teaspoons lime juice

Directions:

1. Take Instant Pot and carefully arrange it over a clean, dry kitchen platform. Turn on the appliance.
2. In the cooking pot area, add the mentioned ingredients except for lime juice and avocado. Stir the ingredients gently.
3. Close the pot lid and seal the valve to avoid any leakage. Find and press "Manual" cooking setting and set cooking time to 25 minutes.
4. Allow the recipe ingredients to cook for the set time, and after that, the timer reads "zero".
5. Press "Cancel" and press "NPR" setting for natural pressure release. It takes 8-10 times for all inside pressure to release.
6. Open the pot, fluff the mixture. Add lime juice and stir.
7. Spoon into bowls. Garnish with avocado slices and serve.

Nutritional Values (Per Serving):

Calories - 461

Fat – 14g

Carbohydrates – 66.5g

Fiber – 11g

Protein – 14g

Avocado Rice Salad

Prep Time: 10min.

Cooking Time: 24 min.

Number of Servings: 6-8

Ingredients:

- 1 can (14 oz.) black beans, drained
- 1 ½ cups water
- ¼ cup cilantro, minced
- 1 cup brown rice
- 1 avocado, diced
- 12 grape tomatoes, make quarters
- ¼ teaspoon salt

For the dressing:

- 2 teaspoons Tabasco (optional)
- 2 garlic cloves, minced
- 3 tablespoons lime juice
- 3 tablespoons extra-virgin olive oil
- 1/ 8 teaspoon salt
- 1 teaspoon maple syrup

Directions:

1. Take Instant Pot and carefully arrange it over a clean, dry kitchen platform. Turn on the appliance.
2. In the cooking pot area, add the rice and water. Stir the ingredients gently.
3. Close the pot lid and seal the valve to avoid any leakage. Find and press "Manual" cooking setting and set cooking time to 24 minutes.
4. Allow the recipe ingredients to cook for the set time, and after that, the timer reads "zero".
5. Press "Cancel" and press "NPR" setting for natural pressure release. It takes 8-10 times for all inside pressure to release.
6. Open the pot and transfer the mixture to the serving container.
7. Mix the black beans, avocado, tomato, and cilantro.

8. In another mixing bowl, whisk the dressing ingredients together. Pour the dressing over the rice mix and combine; serve!

Nutritional Values (Per Serving):

Calories - 376

Fat – 11g

Carbohydrates – 48g

Fiber – 12g

Protein – 14.5g

Spinach Chickpea Rice Meal

Prep Time: 8-10min.

Cooking Time: 25 min.

Number of Servings: 4

Ingredients:

- 1 teaspoon lime juice
- 2 small tomatoes, diced one
- Half inch piece ginger, grated
- ½ teaspoon salt
- 1 tablespoon curry powder
- 1 cup baby spinach
- ½ cup chopped yellow onion
- 2 cups water
- ¼ cup brown rice, cooked
- 1 teaspoon vegetable oil
- 4 garlic cloves, minced
- 1 small acorn squash
- 1 can chickpeas

Directions:

1. Slice squash in half and scrape seeds.
2. Take Instant Pot and carefully arrange it over a clean, dry kitchen platform. Turn on the appliance.
3. Find and press "Sauté" cooking function.
4. In the cooking pot area; add the oil and onions in the pot. Cook for 2-3 minutes to cook well and soften.
5. Add the garlic and cook 1 minute. Mix other ingredients besides squash and cook until spinach is wilted.
6. Place mixture inside each squash half.
7. Pour the water into the cooking pot area. Arrange the trivet inside it; arrange the squash halves over the trivet.
8. Close the pot lid and seal the valve to avoid any leakage. Find and press "Manual" cooking setting and set cooking time to 20 minutes.

9. Allow the recipe ingredients to cook for the set time, and after that, the timer reads "zero".
10. Press "Cancel" and press "NPR" setting for natural pressure release. It takes 8-10 times for all inside pressure to release.
11. Open the pot and arrange the cooked recipe in serving plates. Enjoy the vegan recipe!

Nutritional Values (Per Serving):

Calories –178

Fat – 5g

Carbohydrates – 29.5g

Fiber – 5.5g

Protein – 6g

Sorghum Pumpkin Meal

Prep Time: 5-8min.

Cooking Time: 25 min.

Number of Servings: 5-6

Ingredients:

- 1½ tablespoons pumpkin pie spice
- 1½ cups almond milk, unsweetened
- 1 ½ teaspoons vanilla extract
- 3 tablespoons maple syrup
- 1 ½ cups sorghum, rinsed
- 1 ¼ cups pumpkin puree
- 3 cups water

Directions:

1. Take Instant Pot and carefully arrange it over a clean, dry kitchen platform. Turn on the appliance.
2. In the cooking pot area, add the mentioned ingredients. Stir the ingredients gently.
3. Close the pot lid and seal the valve to avoid any leakage. Find and press "Manual" cooking setting and set cooking time to 25 minutes.
4. Allow the recipe ingredients to cook for the set time, and after that, the timer reads "zero".
5. Press "Cancel" and press "NPR" setting for natural pressure release. It takes 8-10 times for all inside pressure to release.
6. Open the pot and arrange the cooked recipe in serving plates. Serve with almond milk.

Nutritional Values (Per Serving):

Calories - 227

Fat – 2.5g

Carbohydrates – 49.5g

Fiber – 4.5g

Protein – 7g

Spinach Mushroom Risotto

Prep Time: 5min.

Cooking Time: 8 min.

Number of Servings: 5

Ingredients:

- ½ cup white onion, minced
- 4-ounce mushrooms, chopped
- 1 cup Arborio rice
- 1 ½ tablespoon nutritional yeast
- 3 cups vegetable broth
- 2 cups spinach
- ¼ cup lemon juice
- ½ cup dry white wine
- 1 teaspoon salt
- 1 tablespoon vegan butter
- 1 tablespoon olive oil, optional
- 1 teaspoon thyme
- 3 cloves garlic, minced
- Black pepper as needed

Directions:

1. Take Instant Pot and carefully arrange it over a clean, dry kitchen platform. Turn on the appliance.
2. Find and press "Sauté" cooking function.
3. In the cooking pot area; add the oil, garlic, and onions in the pot. Cook for 2 minutes to cook well and soften.
4. Add the rice and stir well. Pour the broth, mushrooms, wine, thyme, and salt.
5. Close the pot lid and seal the valve to avoid any leakage. Find and press "Manual" cooking setting and set cooking time to 5 minutes.
6. Allow the recipe ingredients to cook for the set time, and after that, the timer reads "zero".
7. Press "Cancel" and press "NPR" setting for natural pressure release. It takes 8-10 times for all inside pressure to release.
8. Open the pot and arrange the cooked recipe in serving plates.

9. Mix the yeast, spinach, vegan butter, and pepper. Stir well and serve warm!

Nutritional Values (Per Serving):

Calories - 323

Fat – 8.5g

Carbohydrates – 43.5g

Fiber – 3.5g

Protein – 10g

Green Tea Rice Risotto

Prep Time: 5min.

Cooking Time: 30 min.

Number of Servings: 5-6

Ingredients:

- 1 cup brown rice, rinsed
- ¼ cup lentils, rinsed
- 7 cups water
- 3 green tea bags
- Salt as needed

Directions:

1. Take Instant Pot and carefully arrange it over a clean, dry kitchen platform. Turn on the appliance.
2. In the cooking pot area, add the mentioned ingredients. Stir the ingredients gently.
3. Close the pot lid and seal the valve to avoid any leakage. Find and press "Manual" cooking setting and set cooking time to 30 minutes.
4. Allow the recipe ingredients to cook for the set time, and after that, the timer reads "zero".
5. Press "Cancel" and press "NPR" setting for natural pressure release. It takes 8-10 times for all inside pressure to release.
6. Open the pot, remove tea bags and arrange the cooked recipe in serving plates. Enjoy the vegan recipe!

Nutritional Values (Per Serving):

Calories – 123

Fat – 1g

Carbohydrates – 24.5g

Fiber – 1.5g

Protein – 3g

Chapter 6: Wholesome Vegan Mains

Masala Kidney Beans

Prep Time: 5min.

Cooking Time: 40 min.

Number of Servings: 5-6

Ingredients:

- 1 teaspoon ginger paste
- 1 ½ teaspoons ground cumin
- Chili powder as needed
- 1 teaspoon garlic paste
- 1 teaspoon garam masala
- 2 teaspoons ground coriander
- ½ teaspoon turmeric
- 2 cups dry kidney beans, soaked overnight and drained
- 2 tablespoons vegetable oil
- 2 large onions, chopped
- 3 large tomatoes, chopped
- Water and salt as needed
- Cilantro to garnish

Directions:

1. Take Instant Pot and carefully arrange it over a clean, dry kitchen platform. Turn on the appliance.
2. Find and press "Sauté" cooking function.
3. In the cooking pot area; add the oil and onions in the pot. Cook for 2 minutes to cook well and soften.
4. Add the ginger and garlic pastes and sauté for 2–3 minutes. Add the turmeric, cumin, coriander, garam masala and chili powder and sauté for a few seconds.
5. Add tomatoes and sauté for 2 minutes. Add the kidney beans, stir, and add enough water (2 inches above the ingredients) and salt.
6. Close the pot lid and seal the valve to avoid any leakage. Find and press "Bean/Chili" cooking setting and set cooking time to 30 minutes.

7. Allow the recipe ingredients to cook for the set time, and after that, the timer reads "zero".
8. Press "Cancel" and press "NPR" setting for natural pressure release. It takes 8-10 times for all inside pressure to release.
9. Open the pot. Garnish with cilantro. Serve over rice.

Nutritional Values (Per Serving):

Calories - 292

Fat – 6g

Carbohydrates – 47g

Fiber – 12g

Protein – 15g

Spinach Jalapeno Lentil Curry

Prep Time: 8-10 min.

Cooking Time: 15 min.

Number of Servings: 3

Ingredients:

- 2 medium yellow potatoes, cubed
- 1 jalapeño, diced and seeds removed
- 3 medium tomatoes, diced
- 1 tablespoon curry powder
- 2 teaspoons vegetable oil
- 1 cup baby spinach
- 1 cup water
- ¾ teaspoons salt
- 1/3 cup dry brown lentils
- 4 garlic cloves, minced
- 1-inch piece of ginger, grated

Directions:

1. Soak lentils for one hour.
2. Take Instant Pot and carefully arrange it over a clean, dry kitchen platform. Turn on the appliance.
3. Find and press "Sauté" cooking function.
4. In the cooking pot area; add the oil and onions in the pot. Cook for 3-4 minutes to cook well and soften.
5. Add the ginger, garlic, and pepper. Cook for 2 minutes. Add the tomato, curry powder, water, lentils, and salt.
6. Add the spinach and cook until wilted.
7. Close the pot lid and seal the valve to avoid any leakage. Find and press "Manual" cooking setting and set cooking time to 8 minutes.
8. Allow the recipe ingredients to cook for the set time, and after that, the timer reads "zero".
9. Press "Cancel" and press "NPR" setting for natural pressure release. It takes 8-10 times for all inside pressure to release.

10. Open the pot and arrange the cooked recipe in serving plates. Enjoy the vegan recipe!

Nutritional Values (Per Serving):

Calories – 209

Fat – 4g

Carbohydrates – 36g

Fiber – 11g

Protein – 9.5g

Creamy Lima Beans

Prep Time: 8-10min.

Cooking Time: 15 min.

Number of Servings: 4

Ingredients:

- 1 pound lima beans
- 1 cup sour cream, vegan
- 1 tablespoon dark syrup or your choice such as Karo
- ¾ cup vegan butter
- ¾ brown sugar
- 1 tablespoon dry mustard
- 2 teaspoon salt

Directions:

1. Soak the beans in 10 cups water; add the salt and set aside.
2. In the cooking pot area, add the water and beans. Stir the ingredients gently.
3. Close the pot lid and seal the valve to avoid any leakage. Find and press "Manual" cooking setting and set cooking time to 4 minutes.
4. Allow the recipe ingredients to cook for the set time, and after that, the timer reads "zero".
5. Press "Cancel" and press "NPR" setting for natural pressure release. It takes 8-10 times for all inside pressure to release.
6. Open the pot and drain the beans.
7. Add back in the pot. Add other ingredients and mix gently together.
8. Close the pot lid and seal the valve to avoid any leakage. Find and press "Manual" cooking setting and set cooking time to 10 minutes.
9. Allow the recipe ingredients to cook for the set time, and after that, the timer reads "zero".
10. Press "Cancel" and press "NPR" setting for natural pressure release. It takes 8-10 times for all inside pressure to release.
11. Open the pot and transfer the mixture to serving bowl.

Nutritional Values (Per Serving):

Calories - 397

Fat – 26g

Carbohydrates – 36g

Fiber – 3g

Protein – 4.5g

Zucchini Eggplant Meal

Prep Time: 5min.

Cooking Time: 8 min.

Number of Servings: 6-8

Ingredients:

- 2 cloves minced garlic
- 12 ounces roasted red peppers, make slices
- 1 onion, make thin slices
- 4 zucchini, sliced thin
- 1 can (28 oz.) tomatoes, crushed
- 2 eggplants, peeled and make thin slices
- ½ cup water
- 1 tablespoon olive oil
- 1 teaspoon salt

Directions:

1. Take Instant Pot and carefully arrange it over a clean, dry kitchen platform. Turn on the appliance.
2. Find and press "Sauté" cooking function.
3. Add the zucchini, eggplant, oil, and onion; heat for 2-3 minutes to cook well and soften.
4. Season with the salt and then add the tomatoes and water; stir to combine.
5. Close the pot lid and seal the valve to avoid any leakage. Find and press "Manual" cooking set with 4 minutes cooking time.
6. Allow the recipe ingredients to cook for the set time, and after that, the timer reads "zero".
7. Press "Cancel" and press "NPR" setting for natural pressure release. It takes 8-10 times for all inside pressure to release.
8. Open the pot and arrange the cooked recipe in serving plates. Enjoy the vegan recipe!

Nutritional Values (Per Serving):

Calories - 119

Fat – 2.2g

Carbohydrates – 22g

Fiber – 9.5g

Protein – 5g

Jalapeno Bean Meal

Prep Time: 8-10min.

Cooking Time: 40 min.

Number of Servings: 4

Ingredients:

- ½ pound pinto beans, rinsed
- 2 cloves garlic, minced
- 3 cups water
- ½ teaspoon cumin powder
- 1 small onion, chopped
- ½ tablespoon olive oil
- 1 small jalapeño, chopped
- Salt as needed
- A handful of cilantro, chopped

Directions:

1. Take Instant Pot and carefully arrange it over a clean, dry kitchen platform. Turn on the appliance.
2. Find and press "Sauté" cooking function.
3. In the cooking pot area; add the oil, jalapeno, garlic, and onions in the pot. Cook until turn translucent and soften.
4. Add the beans, cumin, and water. Mix well.
5. Close the pot lid and seal the valve to avoid any leakage. Find and press "Bean/Chili" cooking setting and set cooking time to 30 minutes.
6. Allow the recipe ingredients to cook for the set time, and after that, the timer reads "zero".
7. Press "Cancel" and press "NPR" setting for natural pressure release. It takes 8-10 times for all inside pressure to release.
8. Open the pot, add salt and arrange the cooked recipe in serving plates. Garnish with cilantro and serve.

Nutritional Values (Per Serving):

Calories - 226

Fat – 2.5g

Carbohydrates – 37g

Fiber – 9.5g

Protein – 13g

Wholesome Cauliflower Meal

Prep Time: 8-10min.

Cooking Time: 1 min.

Number of Servings: 4

Ingredients:

- 1 cauliflower head, medium-sized
- 2 tablespoons olive oil
- 2 tablespoons cilantro, chopped
- 1 cup water
- ½ teaspoon dried parsley
- ½ teaspoon salt
- ¼ teaspoon paprika
- ¼ teaspoon ground cumin
- ¼ teaspoon turmeric powder

Directions:

1. Make large pieces of the cauliflower.
2. Take Instant Pot and carefully arrange it over a clean, dry kitchen platform. Turn on the appliance.
3. Pour the water into the cooking pot area. Arrange the trivet inside it; arrange the cauliflower over the trivet.
4. Close the pot lid and seal the valve to avoid any leakage. Find and press "Steam" cooking setting and set cooking time to 1 minutes.
5. Allow the recipe ingredients to cook for the set time, and after that, the timer reads "zero".
6. Press "Cancel" and press "NPR" setting for natural pressure release. It takes 8-10 times for all inside pressure to release.
7. Open the pot and arrange the cooked recipe in serving plates.
8. Empty the pot. Select "Saute". Add the oil and cooked cauliflower; heat for 2 minutes to cook well and soften.
9. Mash it well and mix all the spices; combine and cook for a few minutes. Serve warm!

Nutritional Values (Per Serving):

Calories – 24.5

Fat – 0.5g

Carbohydrates – 5.5g

Fiber – 2.5g

Protein – 2g

Faro Peas Collard Wraps

Prep Time: 5 min.

Cooking Time: 13 min.

Number of Servings: 8

Ingredients:

- 3 tablespoons olive oil
- 1 onion, chopped
- 1 ¼ cups dry black-eyed peas, rinsed
- 6 cloves garlic, minced
- 8 collard green leaves
- 1 teaspoon thyme, dried
- 4 teaspoons soy sauce
- 1 teaspoon dried basil
- 1 1/3 cups faro (semi-pearled), soaked for 30-45 minutes
- 1 teaspoon hot sauce
- Salt as needed
- 2 cups water
- 2 cups broth
- 2 tablespoons oil

Directions:

1. Take Instant Pot and carefully arrange it over a clean, dry kitchen platform. Turn on the appliance.
2. Find and press "Sauté" cooking function.
3. Add the oil and farro; heat for 2-3 minutes to cook well and soften. Add other ingredients except for broth and collard; cook for a few more minutes.
4. Add the broth and stir.
5. Close the pot lid and seal the valve to avoid any leakage. Find and press "Manual" cooking setting and set cooking time to 10 minutes.
6. Allow the recipe ingredients to cook for the set time, and after that, the timer reads "zero".
7. Press "Cancel" and press "NPR" setting for natural pressure release. It takes 8-10 times for all inside pressure to release.
8. Place the collard on a platform. Spread the mixture over them, roll and serve.

Nutritional Values (Per Serving):

Calories – 343

Fat – 10g

Carbohydrates – 38.5g

Fiber – 6g

Protein – 14.5g

Chili Bean Tacos

Prep Time: 8-10min.

Cooking Time: 40 min.

Number of Servings: 5-6

Ingredients:

- 1 teaspoon salt
- 2 tablespoons tomato paste
- ½ teaspoon cumin
- 2 teaspoons chili powder
- 2 teaspoons oregano
- 1 small onion, chopped
- 3 cups water
- 1 pound dried chili beans, plus extra water
- 6 taco shells or tortillas
- 1 bell pepper, minced
- 2 garlic cloves, chopped

Directions:

1. Take Instant Pot and carefully arrange it over a clean, dry kitchen platform. Turn on the appliance.
2. Find and press "Sauté" cooking function. Fill the pot with water to come above the surface of the beans and boil.
3. Boil the mix 5 minutes. Drain.
4. Put the beans back in the pot. Add the chili powder, oregano, cumin, garlic, and onion.
5. Close the pot lid and seal the valve to avoid any leakage. Find and press "Manual" cooking setting and set cooking time to 5 minutes.
6. Allow the recipe ingredients to cook for the set time, and after that, the timer reads "zero".
7. Press "Cancel" and press "NPR" setting for natural pressure release. It takes 8-10 times for all inside pressure to release.
8. Open and add remaining ingredients. Cook uncovered 30 minutes.

9. Serve the mix on taco shells.

Nutritional Values (Per Serving):

Calories –249

Fat – 5g

Carbohydrates – 38.5gs

Fiber – 4g

Protein – 9.5g

Chapter 7: Savory Vegan Snacks

Oregano Black Bean

Prep Time: 5-8min.

Cooking Time: 20 min.

Number of Servings: 6

Ingredients:

- 15 cherry tomatoes, sliced in half
- 1 teaspoon coriander
- 1 teaspoon oregano
- ½ teaspoon chili flakes
- 1 teaspoon cumin
- 1 teaspoon sea salt
- 2 tablespoons vegetable oil
- 1 teaspoon paprika
- 1 ½ cups dry black beans
- 3 garlic cloves, minced
- 1 large yellow onion
- 2 cubes vegetable bouillon

Directions:

1. Take Instant Pot and carefully arrange it over a clean, dry kitchen platform. Turn on the appliance.
2. In the cooking pot area; add beans and water to the pressure cooker and dissolve in bouillon cubes.
3. Close the pot lid and seal the valve to avoid any leakage. Find and press "Manual" cooking setting and set cooking time to 15 minutes.
4. Allow the recipe ingredients to cook for the set time and after that, the timer reads "zero".
5. Press "Cancel" and press "NPR" setting for natural pressure release. It takes 8-10 times for all inside pressure to release.
6. Open the pot and remove beans from the pot.

7. Place oil in the pot and using sauté setting, cook onion 3 minutes. Add garlic and cook 1 minute.
8. Put all remaining ingredients including the beans in the pot. Stir gently.
9. Close the pot lid and seal the valve to avoid any leakage. Find and press "Manual" cooking setting and set cooking time to 1 minutes.
10. Allow the recipe ingredients to cook for the set time, and after that, the timer reads "zero".
11. Press "Cancel" and press "NPR" setting for natural pressure release. It takes 8-10 times for all inside pressure to release.
12. Open the pot and arrange the cooked recipe in serving plates. Enjoy the vegan recipe!

Nutritional Values (Per Serving):

Calories - 356

Fat – 11g

Carbohydrates – 41.5g

Fiber – 12g

Protein – 28g

Classic Potato Fries

Prep Time: 5min.

Cooking Time: 10-15 min.

Number of Servings: 8

Ingredients:

- 2 pounds russet potatoes, peeled and slice to make fries
- 1/2 teaspoon baking soda
- 2 teaspoons kosher salt
- Canola oil to deep fry as needed
- 2 cups cold water

Directions:

1. Take Instant Pot and carefully arrange it over a clean, dry kitchen platform. Turn on the appliance.
2. Pour the water, soda and, salt in the cooking pot area. Arrange the trivet inside it; arrange the potatoes over the trivet.
3. Close the pot lid and seal the valve to avoid any leakage. Find and press "Manual" cooking setting and set cooking time to 2 minutes.
4. Allow the recipe ingredients to cook for the set time, and after that, the timer reads "zero".
5. Press "Cancel" and press "NPR" setting for natural pressure release. It takes 8-10 times for all inside pressure to release.
6. Open the pot and take out the fries.
7. Take a deep frying pan and add in the oil to a half depth of the pan size. Heat the pan over medium heat.
8. Add the fries in batches and fry until it is light golden brown. Enjoy the fries!

Nutritional Values (Per Serving):

Calories –168

Fat – 0g

Carbohydrates – 38g

Fiber – 3g

Protein – 5g

Chickpea Hummus

Prep Time: 5min.

Cooking Time: 10 min.

Number of Servings: 5-6

Ingredients:

- 1 tablespoon hot sauce of choice
- 1 tablespoon lemon juice
- 1 teaspoon salt
- 1 teaspoon black pepper
- ½ teaspoon smoked paprika
- 1 cup dry chickpeas, rinsed
- 3-4 tablespoons tahini
- 3 garlic cloves
- 3 cups water

Directions:

1. Take Instant Pot and carefully arrange it over a clean, dry kitchen platform. Turn on the appliance.
2. In the cooking pot area, add the beans and water.
3. Close the pot lid and seal the valve to avoid any leakage. Find and press "Manual" cooking setting and set cooking time to 10 minutes.
4. Allow the recipe ingredients to cook for the set time, and after that, the timer reads "zero". Press "Cancel" and press "NPR" setting for natural pressure release. It takes 8-10 times for all inside pressure to release.
5. Open the pot. Add chickpeas and garlic to food processor and pulse to form a crumbly mix. Add other ingredients and pulse to combine.
6. Gradually add water to get the desired consistency. Serve, or also you can refrigerate, and use it later.

Nutritional Values (Per Serving):

Calories –114

Fat – 7g

Carbohydrates – 9g

Fiber – 3g

Protein – 5.5g

Soy Sauce Tofu

Prep Time: 10min.

Cooking Time: 2 ½ hour

Number of Servings: 2

Ingredients:

- 1/2 tablespoon apple cider vinegar
- 1 tablespoon soy sauce
- 1/4 teaspoon garlic powder
- 1/4 teaspoon salt
- 1 container extra firm tofu, prepare 1-inch cubes
- 1/2 tablespoon red pepper flakes
- 3/4 cup ketchup
- 1 1/2 tablespoon brown sugar

Directions:

1. Take Instant Pot and carefully arrange it over a clean, dry kitchen platform. Turn on the appliance.
2. In the cooking pot area, add the mentioned ingredients. Stir the ingredients gently.
3. Close the pot lid and seal the valve to avoid any leakage. Find and press "Slow cook" cooking setting and set cooking time to 2 hours 30 minutes.
4. Allow the recipe ingredients to cook for the set time, and after that, the timer reads "zero".
5. Press "Cancel" and press "NPR" setting for natural pressure release. It takes 8-10 times for all inside pressure to release.
6. Cook for more time in the mix is too watery.
7. Open the pot and arrange the cooked recipe in serving plates. Enjoy the vegan recipe!

Nutritional Values (Per Serving):

Calories - 246

Fat – 4g

Carbohydrates – 21g

Fiber – 3g

Protein – 11.5g

Chapter 8: Vegan Sauces & Spreads

Apple Mango Spread/Chutney

Prep Time: 5min.

Cooking Time: 7 min.

Number of Servings: Makes 2 cups

Ingredients:

- 1 apple, core removed and chopped
- 2 mangoes, diced
- 1 tablespoon ginger, grated
- 1 shallot, sliced thinly
- ½ teaspoon red pepper flakes
- 1 tablespoon vegetable oil
- 1 ¼ cups apple cider vinegar
- 1 ¼ cups sugar
- 2 teaspoons salt
- Pinch of cinnamon
- Pinch of cardamom powder

Directions:

1. Take Instant Pot and carefully arrange it over a clean, dry kitchen platform. Turn on the appliance.
2. Find and press "Sauté" cooking function.
3. In the cooking pot area; add the oil, shallots, and ginger in the pot. Cook for 2 minutes to cook well and soften.
4. Add spices and stir, cooking for 10 seconds. Add everything else and stir until sugar dissolves.
5. Close the pot lid and seal the valve to avoid any leakage. Find and press "Manual" cooking setting and set cooking time to 7 minutes.
6. Allow the recipe ingredients to cook for the set time, and after that, the timer reads "zero".
7. Press "Cancel" and press "NPR" setting for natural pressure release. It takes 8-10 times for all inside pressure to release.

8. Open lid, and using sauté setting, continue cooking until the mix turns thick. Transfer to the jar, cool down and then refrigerate until use.

Nutritional Values (Per Serving):

Calories - 163

Fat – 2g

Carbohydrates – 42.5g

Fiber – 2g

Protein – 1g

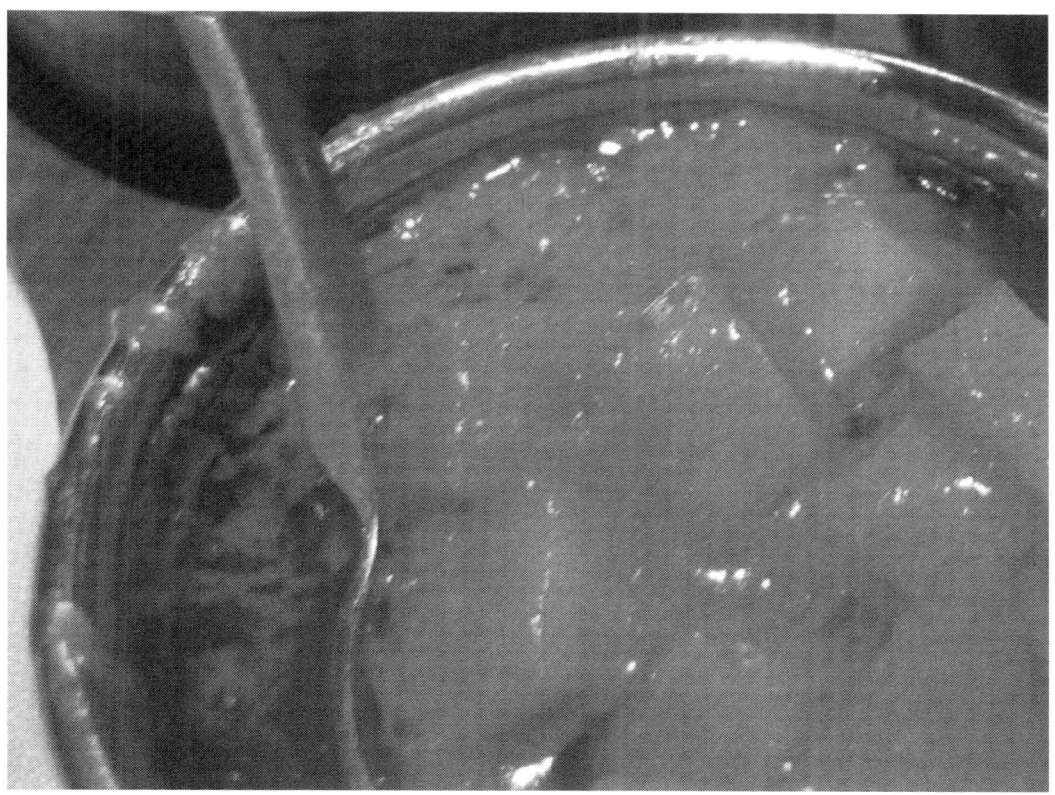

BBQ Sauce

Prep Time: 5-8min.

Cooking Time: 13-15 min.

Number of Servings: Makes 2 ½ cups

Ingredients:

- 1 teaspoon hot sauce of choice
- 1 teaspoon liquid smoke
- ¾ cup dried prunes
- ¼ teaspoon cumin
- ¼ cup agave or maple syrup
- ¼ teaspoon garlic powder
- ½ cup water
- ¼ cup apple cider vinegar
- 1 teaspoon salt
- 1 medium onion, chopped
- 1 tablespoon vegetable oil
- ½ cup tomato puree

Directions:

1. Take Instant Pot and carefully arrange it over a clean, dry kitchen platform. Turn on the appliance.
2. Find and press "Sauté" cooking function.
3. In the cooking pot area; add the oil and onions in the pot. Cook for 2 minutes to cook well and soften.
4. Mix the vinegar, syrup, tomato puree and water and mix well until syrup is dissolved.
5. Add hot sauce and spices, then add the prunes.
6. Close the pot lid and seal the valve to avoid any leakage. Find and press "Manual" cooking setting and set cooking time to 10 minutes.
7. Allow the recipe ingredients to cook for the set time, and after that, the timer reads "zero". Press "Cancel" and press "QPR" setting for quick pressure release.
8. Open the pot and puree the mixture, then pour into glass bottles and seal.
9. Once cooled, store in the refrigerator, and use later as needed!

Nutritional Values (Per Serving):

Calories - 72

Fat – 2g

Carbohydrates – 21.5g

Fiber – 2.5g

Protein – 2g

Garlic Tomato Sauce

Prep Time: 5min.

Cooking Time: 45 min.

Number of Servings: Makes 6-7 cups

Ingredients:

- 1 medium onion, chopped
- 2 tablespoons vegetable oil
- 7 cups can diced tomatoes
- 2 carrots, diced cayenne
- 6 garlic cloves, minced
- Pepper and salt
- ¼ cup chopped fresh herbs

Directions:

1. Take Instant Pot and carefully arrange it over a clean, dry kitchen platform. Turn on the appliance.
2. Find and press "Sauté" cooking function.
3. In the cooking pot area; add the oil and onions in the pot. Cook for 3-4 minutes to cook well and soften.
4. Add the garlic and cook 1 minute. Add everything else.
5. Close the pot lid and seal the valve to avoid any leakage. Find and press "Manual" cooking setting and set cooking time to 45 minutes.
6. Allow the recipe ingredients to cook for the set time, and after that, the timer reads "zero". Press "Cancel" and press "QPR" setting for quick pressure release.
7. Open the pot. Add Pepper and salt and cayenne, if necessary and serve.

Nutritional Values (Per Serving):

Calories –42

Fat – 3g

Carbohydrates – 5g

Fiber – 1g

Protein – 1.5g

Pumpkin Butter

Prep Time: 5min.

Cooking Time: 3 min.

Number of Servings: Makes 3 cups

Ingredients:

- 1 teaspoon cinnamon
- Pinch of clove
- ½ cup sugar
- Pinch allspice
- Pinch nutmeg
- 1 cup apple juice
- 1 teaspoon ground ginger
- 2 can pumpkin puree

Directions:

1. Take Instant Pot and carefully arrange it over a clean, dry kitchen platform. Turn on the appliance.
2. In the cooking pot area, add the mentioned ingredients. Stir the ingredients gently.
3. Close the pot lid and seal the valve to avoid any leakage. Find and press "Manual" cooking setting and set cooking time to 3 minutes.
4. Allow the recipe ingredients to cook for the set time, and after that, the timer reads "zero".
5. Press "Cancel" and press "NPR" setting for natural pressure release. It takes 8-10 times for all inside pressure to release.
6. Open the pot. Pour into jars, seal and let cool. You can store in the fridge one week.

Nutritional Values (Per Serving):

Calories –55

Fat – 2g

Carbohydrates – 14.5g

Fiber – 2g

Protein – 0.5g

Chapter 9: Delicious Desserts

Cashew Tapioca Pudding

Prep Time: 5-8min.

Cooking Time: 10 min.

Number of Servings: 5-6

Ingredients:

- ½ cup maple syrup
- ½ cup tapioca pearls, soaked for at least 1 hour
- 3 tablespoons chopped cashews
- 1 cups coconut milk
- Some lemon zest
- 6 roasted cashews for garnishing

Directions:

1. Take Instant Pot and carefully arrange it over a clean, dry kitchen platform. Turn on the appliance.
2. In the cooking pot area, add the tapioca pearls, coconut milk, maple syrup, chopped cashews, and lemon zest. Stir the ingredients gently.
3. Close the pot lid and seal the valve to avoid any leakage. Find and press "Manual" cooking setting and set cooking time to 10 minutes.
4. Allow the recipe ingredients to cook for the set time, and after that, the timer reads "zero".
5. Press "Cancel" and press "NPR" setting for natural pressure release. It takes 8-10 times for all inside pressure to release.
6. Open the pot. Serve chilled with roasted cashews on top.

Nutritional Values (Per Serving):

Calories - 238

Fat – 12g

Carbohydrates – 32.5g

Fiber – 1.2g

Protein – 2g

Stuffed Dessert Apples

Prep Time: 5min.

Cooking Time: 10 min.

Number of Servings: 6

Ingredients:

- 4 tablespoons maple syrup
- ½ cup cranberries
- 6 medium apples
- ½ cup walnuts, chopped
- ½ teaspoon ground cinnamon
- 1 cup water
- Some cashews, roasted and chopped
- ¼ teaspoon ground nutmeg

Directions:

1. Leave the bottom part of the apples as it is and core the apples. Slowly scoop out some more pulp from inside.
2. In a mixing bowl, mix rest of the ingredients except the cashews, and fill the mixture inside the apple.
3. Add water to the Instant Pot. Add the apples to the pot with bottom part resting on the surface of the pot.
4. Close the pot lid and seal the valve to avoid any leakage. Find and press "Manual" cooking setting and set cooking time to 10 minutes.
5. Allow the recipe ingredients to cook for the set time, and after that, the timer reads "zero".
6. Press "Cancel" and press "NPR" setting for natural pressure release. It takes 8-10 times for all inside pressure to release.
7. Open the pot. Sprinkle with cashews and serve hot.

Nutritional Values (Per Serving):

Calories - 223

Fat – 6.5g

Carbohydrates – 41.5g

Fiber – 6.5g

Protein – 3g

Berry Dessert Mystery

Prep Time: 5 min.

Cooking Time: 2 min.

Number of Servings: 7-8

Ingredients:

- 4 cups blackberries or blueberries
- 4 cups raspberries or strawberries, divide into halves
- 4 tablespoons lemon juice
- 4 tablespoons maple syrup or sweetener of your choice

Directions:

1. Take Instant Pot and carefully arrange it over a clean, dry kitchen platform. Turn on the appliance.
2. In the cooking pot area, add the strawberries, maple syrup, lemon juice and ⅓ of the blueberries. Stir the ingredients gently.
3. Close the pot lid and seal the valve to avoid any leakage. Find and press "Manual" cooking setting and set cooking time to 2 minutes.
4. Allow the recipe ingredients to cook for the set time, and after that, the timer reads "zero".
5. Press "Cancel" and press "NPR" setting for natural pressure release. It takes 8-10 times for all inside pressure to release.
6. Open the pot and chill in the refrigerator. Serve chilled!

Nutritional Values (Per Serving):

Calories – 96

Fat – 0.5g

Carbohydrates – 23g

Fiber – 3.5g

Protein – 1.5g

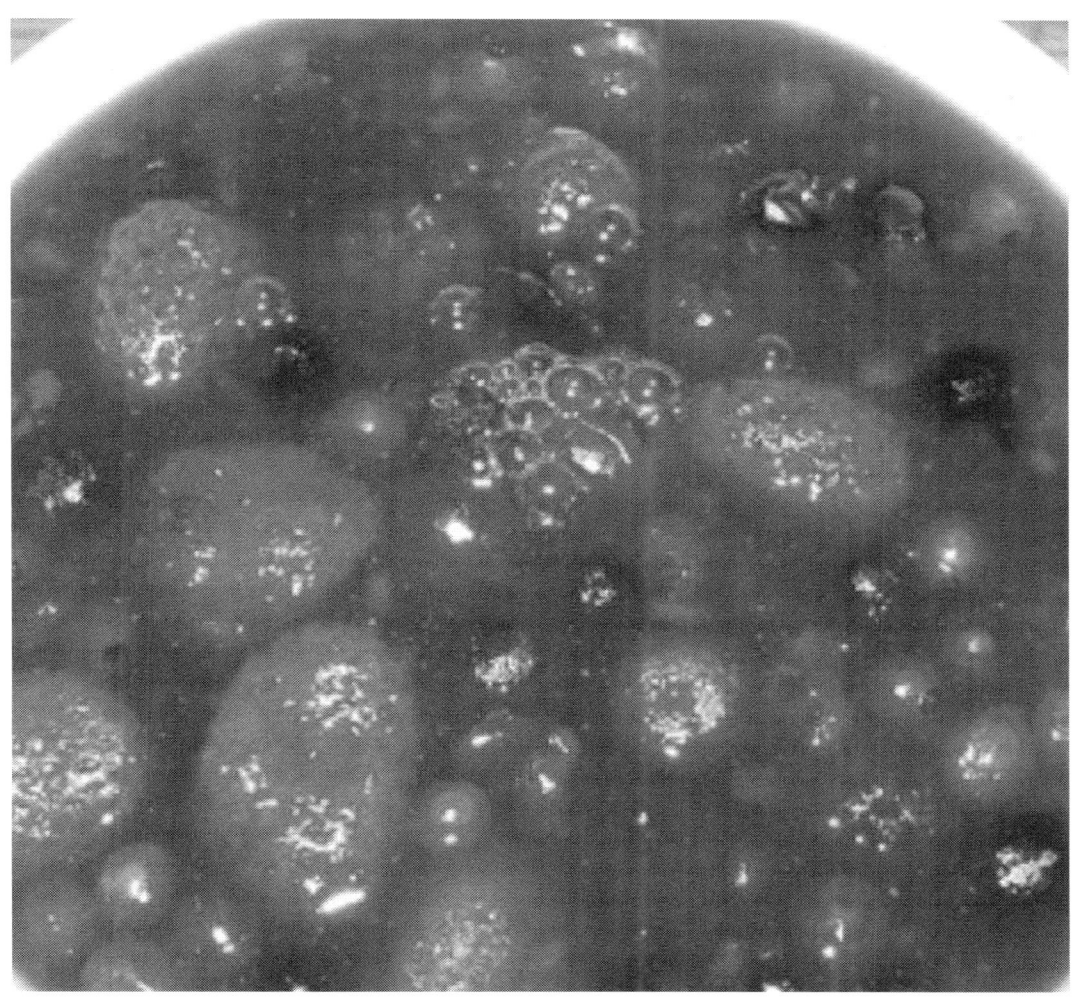

Buckwheat Banana Treat

Prep Time: 5-8min.

Cooking Time: 8 min.

Number of Servings: 7-8

Ingredients:

- 2 teaspoons ground cinnamon
- 6 cups rice milk
- 2 cups buckwheat groats, rinsed
- 2 bananas, sliced
- ½ cup raisins
- 1 teaspoon vanilla extract
- Chopped nuts for garnishing

Directions:

1. Take Instant Pot and carefully arrange it over a clean, dry kitchen platform. Turn on the appliance.
2. In the cooking pot area, add the mentioned ingredients. Stir the ingredients gently.
3. Close the pot lid and seal the valve to avoid any leakage. Find and press "Manual" cooking setting and set cooking time to 8 minutes.
4. Allow the recipe ingredients to cook for the set time, and after that, the timer reads "zero".
5. Press "Cancel" and press "NPR" setting for natural pressure release. It takes 8-10 times for all inside pressure to release.
6. Open the pot and arrange the cooked recipe in serving plates. Garnish with nuts and serve.

Nutritional Values (Per Serving):

Calories - 243

Fat – 2.5g

Carbohydrates – 53.5g

Fiber – 4g

Protein – 4.5g

Conclusion

Instant Pot is a good investment for the money spent; it is one in all kitchen appliance that takes care of all your cooking worries. You can also cook food in batches and freeze them for later usage; just take out the frozen meal and reheat in an oven for a ready, warm vegan meal.

Cooking your favorite vegan meals has never been easier. It is easy to operate and saves you from spending hours in the kitchen. With Instant Pot, you can have nutrient-rich food at home every day along with their mesmerizing deliciousness.

We sincerely hope that the book has succeeded in its aim to educate the readers about creative ways to make delicious Instant Pot Vegan cuisines at home. We ascertain that the versatile recipes covered in the book will help all its readers to transform their everyday diet and lead a quality lifestyle.

Vegan cooking allows freedom with ingredients, and you can surely experiment with your favorite ingredients while cooking these recipes. Let your creativity shine and add your own touch to these recipes to make your customized version.

Thank you and have a great time enjoying the delicious recipes!

Made in the USA
San Bernardino, CA
30 December 2018